AMERICAN INDIAN FAMILIES

A TRUE BOOK

by

Jay Miller

Children's Press®

A Division of Grolier Publishing

New York London Hong Kong Sydney
Danbury, Connecticut

For help in reading and writing these books, Jay Miller thanks Tamaya, Garrett, Erica, and Aaron.

Reading Consultant
Linda Cornwell
Learning Resource Consultant
Indiana Department of Education

Library of Congress Cataloging-in-Publication Data

Miller, Jay, 1947-
    American Indian families / by Jay Miller.
        p.   cm. — (A true book)
    Includes bibliographical references and index.
    Summary: Introduces the different kinds of family relationships among American Indians and how they varied from one tribe to another.
    ISBN 0-516-20133-6 (lib. bdg.)   ISBN 0-516-26089-8 (pbk.)
    1. Indians of North America—Kinship—Juvenile literature. 2. Indians of North America—Social life and customs—Juvenile literature. 3. Family—United States—Juvenile literature. 4. Social structure—United States—Juvenile literature. [1. Indians of North America—Social life and customs. 2. Family.] I. Title. II. Series.
E98.K48M55 1996
306.85'08997—dc20   96-15164
                                                                            CIP
                                                                            AC

13 14 15 16 17 18 19 20 R 10 09 08 07 06

Contents

A Navajo family shelters from the sun.

Names Are Important

For American Indians, family is the most important thing in life. Names are important, too, because they give people an identity and say who their ancestors are.

Families and names can affect who someone marries, how they grow up, and even how they talk.

Some American Indians still use special terms to talk to or about their relatives. This practice comes from a time when people thought a person's name was too sacred to be used in public. Often, these terms meant more than one person and that a person had many "mothers" and "fathers."

Among the Delaware, "gahes" meant not only the woman who gave birth to a child but also all of the woman's sisters. The father of the child, and each of the father's brothers, was called "nok."

People older than a child's parents were called "grandmother" or "grandfather."

A grandmother carries her granddaughter.

They raised the children while the parents were busy getting food for the family and making what they needed to survive.

To show respect, people also gave kin terms to all of the important things in their world. Fire might be called "grandfather." The sun was "father," and Earth "mother" or "grandmother."

Arctic Ocean

Inuit

Inuit

Inuit

Northwest

Pacific Ocean

Kootenay

Cheyenne

Lakota **Plains**

Arapaho

Mohawk

Delaware

Hopi

Navajo Pueblo

Southwest

Apache

Southeast

Atlantic Ocean

NORTH AMERICAN
TRIBES

Seminole

Gulf of Mexico

Caribbean Sea

Families

In Indian society, people could belong to several groups. The smallest was the family. Everyone who ate together around one fire was considered a family. Married couples and their children made up the center of the family. Sometimes, an important man had more than

Families do many things together— from singing at a picnic to cutting firewood.

one wife. Their children were raised together. During hard times, when people were few, women might have several husbands, but this was rare.

In the West and North of North America, some tribes lived by gathering seeds, nuts, berries, and roots, and by hunting animals. Each family had a tent or house that could be moved so they could go to new sources of food. Families were small—a married couple, their young children, and an older relative or two. Each family belonged to larger groups of kin called bands. A band included everyone on both sides of the

Many Mohawk families lived in a longhouse.

family. Each band shared a language, customs, and land.

Elsewhere, farmers and other tribes with abundant food lived in large permanent houses with many fires and families inside. During feasts and ceremonies everyone in the house used the same fire and ate together.

13

Bigger than Families

People in farming tribes belonged to groups of relatives that were much larger in number than individual families. They were called clans. Clan members shared the same ancestor. Clans still exist today.

Some tribes traced their ancestor through their mother's

An Arapaho great-grandmother with her family— daughter, granddaughter, and great-granddaughter.

relatives. In these tribes, fathers were not in charge of their own children. Instead, the oldest brother of the mother helped raise her children. Why is that? Because the mother, her children, and her brothers were related to each other through the mother and the mother's mother, but the father was not.

The father was related to his own mother and sisters. He taught and trained his own sister's children.

The ancestor of a clan might be a human, but more often it was a spirit who showed special concern for these related fami-

Clans were named after many things, such as the sun and buffalo.

lies. The clan was named after its spirit ancestor. Examples of such names are the Sun, Pine, Flint, Ivy, and Buffalo clans.

A Northwest Coast House was home to people descended from the same ancestor.

Along the Pacific Coast from what is now Canada to California, a special kind of clan exists. It is called the

House, but it is more than just a building. A House is composed of all those people descended from the same spirit or human ancestor.

Other cultures have a similar idea. For example, the Queen of England belongs to the House of Windsor. Each Samurai warrior in Japan belonged to an ancestral house. In the Bible, Jesus belonged to the House of David.

Babies

Much of a family's time was spent raising its children, so that the family would continue.

Families were careful when a baby was coming. Spirits were everywhere, and people needed their help to do any-thing well, including having a baby. To show the spirits she wished for an easy delivery, a

A Cheyenne
mother and baby

pregnant woman never stood
in a doorway or blocked a
passage. Other family
members ate carefully so that
the baby would be healthy.

After the baby was born,
mother and newborn remained

apart from everyone else for a certain number of days. Sometimes, a mother and son stayed inside for eight days. A mother and daughter stayed for five days. Sometimes the father did the same to show that he was willing to take on the duties of fatherhood.

In very important families, the baby was named when it and the mother returned to the community. Children of other families were not given a name until they were older.

Often, the father's older sister helped with the naming ceremony and made a cradleboard for the baby. Every tribe had its own style of cradleboard to show if the baby was a boy or a girl.

The baby on the left is in a Navajo cradleboard. Babies could sleep in little hammocks when they weren't being carried (below).

Children

Children grew up surrounded by loving relatives. They learned to do what adults did. And they learned the ways of plants and animals. One of the first things they learned was how to find food. In the Great Lakes region, children gathered cranberries because the thin bogs could not support the weight of grown-ups.

By playing with a puppy, an Inuit girl gets to know a future sled dog.

Children surrounded by their family at a summer camp

Important families had parties every time their children did something for the first time. The first meat, step, or spoken word were celebrated. The Navajo had a party for the first laugh and the Kootenay people for the first whistle. An important milestone came when a boy killed his first animal during a hunt or a girl brought home her first berry or crop.

When boys and girls were old enough, their families sent them to find a spirit who would help them all life long. They had to pray and not eat or drink anything. After a few days

A father helps his son get ready for a powwow.

a spirit who looked like a person came and told what kind of help it would give. In this way, a person became a carver, potter, singer, or basket maker. Natural ability was not enough. To be a success, someone had to have a spirit helper.

Another big event was coming of age, when boys and girls started to become adults. In ancient times, these changes indicated they were ready for marriage.

BECOMING A WOMAN

When a girl's body starts to change and grow into a woman's, or a boy's body grow into a man's, this is *a time of celebration*. Soon they will be adults, and will make families of their own. American Indian people have always celebrated this important time, and this tradition continues today.

As part of her ceremony, an Apache girl dances with a friend while men sing the creation story behind her.

She lies on the earth and is molded like the earth is molded, so that she will have the power of the earth.

She is blessed with sacred pollen. Other rites are performed. Now she is ready to become a woman.

Marriage

In many American Indian tribes, elders arranged children's marriages, because this decision was too important to be left to the youngsters themselves. Yet, the children's wishes were respected. Usually, they didn't have to marry someone they did not like.

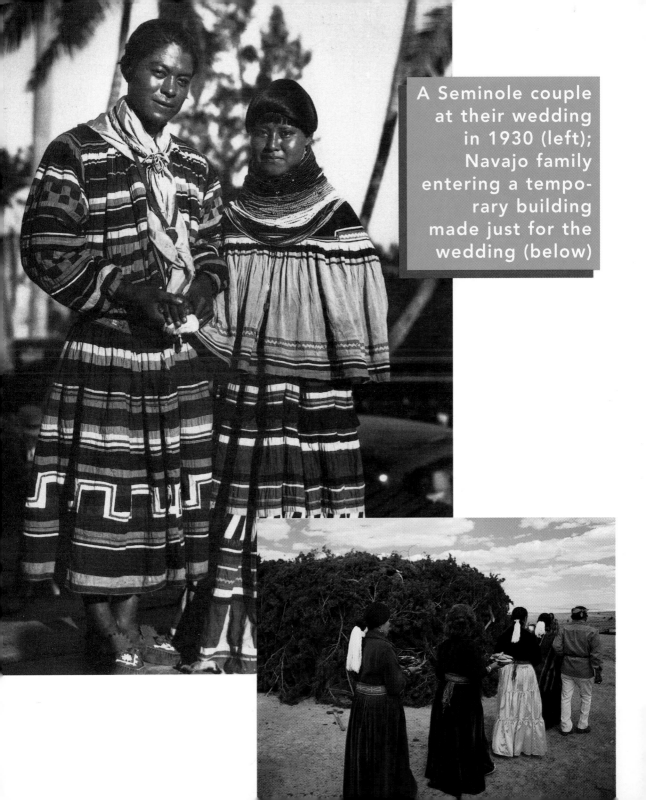

A Seminole couple at their wedding in 1930 (left); Navajo family entering a temporary building made just for the wedding (below)

The married couple moved in with one of their families. If the children traced their ancestry through the mother, then the newlyweds lived with the bride's family. If ancestry was traced through the father, then the couple lived with the groom's family.

Great respect was shown to the in-laws. Among the Apache, a son-in-law showed this regard by avoiding his mother-in-law. He could not speak to her or be

Wedding cakes are a new tradition.

alone with her. If he had to tell her something, he spoke to someone or something nearby. A daughter-in-law also avoided her husband's parents, but since she cooked and kept the house for them, she did not ignore them totally. Some of these customs are still being practiced today.

Other relatives were treated differently. For example, sisters-in-law and brothers-in-law could be friendly and joke together because they were close in age.

Throughout married life, people worked hard and contributed to their camp or town. They were expected to think of others first and uphold the family honor.

Growing Old

Everyone hoped to grow old and die surrounded by family. As people got older, they became more religious. They prayed and gave offerings to the spirits. They wanted their family to be well and happy.

Elders prepared for their death. They had fine clothes

An elder

ready to wear for burial. They gave away possessions to their family and friends. The wisest elders had special knowledge. They trained heirs to take their places, and passed on their knowledge to them.

After death, the body was washed and dressed. For several days, everyone gathered to say goodbye to the person who had died.

Usually tribes followed differ-ent customs with the body. The Cheyenne placed their dead in

Burial grounds, such as this Hopi one, are holy places.

trees. Eventually, the remains were buried.

Usually, chiefs were buried in a place overlooking their people. Doctors were buried away from towns. In death, they were too powerful to keep nearby. Only their relatives visited their graves.

The person's spirit went to a place where all the tribe's ancestors lived. There, its relatives welcomed it.

Today, many American Indians still hold these beliefs. They believe that the living and the dead can visit because they are related.

A memorial powwow honors the dead.

Related to All Things

American Indians believe that everything in life is related and remains connected even after death. That is why they show great respect for life and believe that everything has a special place and purpose that should be shared.

A grandmother helps her grandchild at a powwow.

The Lakota Sioux refer to this important relationship. Often, they pray, "mitakuye oyasin"—we are all related!

To Find Out More

Here are some additional resources to help you learn more about American Indian families:

 Books

 Videos

Rendon, Marcie R. **Powwow Summer: A Family Celebrates the Circle of Life.** Lerner Publications, 1996.

Swentzell, Rina. **Children of Clay: A Family of Pueblo Potters.** Lerner Publications, 1992.

Wolfson, Evelyn. **Growing up Indian.** Walker and Co., 1986.

Wood, Ted, with Wanbli Numpa Afraid of Hawk. **A Boy Becomes a Man at Wounded Knee.** Walker and Co., 1995.

Charles, Tony, director. **I Am Different from My Brother.** Native American Public Broadcasting Consortium, 1981.

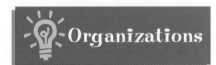 **Organizations**

American Indian Community House, Inc.
404 Lafayette Street
New York, NY
212-598-0100

American Indian Heritage Foundation
6051 Arlington Blvd.
Falls Church, VA 22044
202-463-4267

Online Sites

Aboriginal Youth Network
http://ayn-0.ayn.ca/

This Canadian site is for young people of all cultures.

Index of Native American Resources on the Internet
http://hanksville.phast. umass.edu/misc/ NAresources.html

Start here to find resources on every aspect of American Indian life and culture.

NativeWeb Home Page
http://web.maxwell.syr.edu/ nativeweb/

This is another excellent starting point, and connection to information about indigenous people all over the world.

Important Words

ancestors relatives from long ago

band a group of related families that share a leader and ancestors

cradleboards baby carriers

culture ideas, actions, and habits that children learn as they grow up in a certain group of people

elder a wise older person

house families from the same ancestor sharing a building

ritual an action that is always done in a certain way as part of an important event

spirit invisible beings with power over the natural world

traditions ancient customs and beliefs

Index

Meet the Author

Jay Miller lives in Seattle, visiting nearby reservations, mountains, streams, and the Pacific Ocean. He enjoys eating salmon and pie, hiking in the mountains, and kayaking along the shore as much as he enjoys being a writer, professor, and lecturer. He has taught in colleges in the United States and Canada. He belongs to the Delaware Wolf clan. His family is delightful and very complex. He has also authored *American Indian Games*, *American Indian Festivals*, and *American Indian Foods* for the True Book series.